# Gambling With Grace:
# A Journey to Freedom

By: Ben Ellard

GAMBLING WITH GRACE

© 2011 by Ben Ellard

ISBN-13: 978-1463622046
ISBN-10: 146362204X

Cover design by Tasha York
Interior by Bluegrass Creative

Unless otherwise indicated, Scripture quotations are from:
*The New American Standard Bible (NASB)*
© 1971, 1995, The Lockman Foundation

No part of this publication may be reproduced, stored in a retrieval system, or transmitted, in any form or by any means - electronic, mechanical, photocopying, recording, or otherwise - without prior written permission.

For information visit www.benellard.net

*I am not a Bible scholar, nor do I claim to be. I am just an ordinary man that realized he was in desperate need of a Savior.*

Dedicated to Bud Pierson, my dear friend.

# Acknowledgments

To God: Thanks for everything You have done in me, to me, and through me. I love You.

To my parents: Thank you for loving me through my goofiness and weirdness. I love you more today than yesterday. You are my best friends, parents, and siblings in Christ. God absolutely blessed me with you guys.

To Rusty Kennedy: Thank you for being sensitive to the Holy Spirit and letting Him work through you to teach me my true identity. It's been a life changer.

To Pam McCardwell: You are missed so much. You were the first person to ever manifest grace to me. Thank you for that. Hug our Heavenly Father for me.

To Jody Graham: Thank you for your friendship and community where I can be open and free to be who our Creator wired me to be. It means more than you know.

To Mike Newton: A close friend of mine from the early years till now. Thank you for your friendship. It means more to me than you may realize.

To Keaton Kershner: Such an authentic person. Thank you for allowing me to know you and, in turn, be known by you.

To Melissa Goble: Thank you so much for you help, time and effort in making this possible. The time and energy you've given is remarkable and can not go unnoticed - thank you.

To Ed Goble: A man of God and close friend.

To the crew at Huddle House in Campbellsville, Kentucky (nothing like a product placement here): I have inhabited your late night diner for the past year as I comprised this book. You guys might as well be my family. Thank you for the biscuits, Pepsi, and friendship.

To my friends and family: I'm forever grateful for you.

To John Lynch: Amazing mentor, friend, and an authentic man of God. Thank you for your support and affirmation.

Finally, to Bud Pierson: Many late nights have we had over the years talking inside your tattoo shop. I will always cherish those moments of jokes, stories, and conversations. I consider you my best friend. Your friendship, to me, is like eating chocolate cake without getting fat or high cholesterol. Love you man

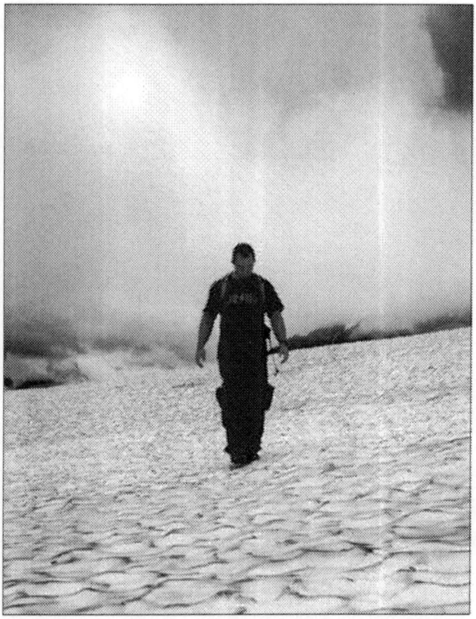

# Table of Contents

Forward ................................................................. 10

Introduction ......................................................... 15

The Cross ............................................................. 21

The Beauty of Covenant ................................... 25

Loving to Death .................................................. 40

Sufficient Forgiveness ....................................... 46

The Heart of Love ............................................... 53

The Gift of No Condemnation .......................... 57

Jesus ...................................................................... 61

Function of the Holy Spirit ............................... 67

God Does Not Need Me ..................................... 82

Theology or Environment ................................. 87

The Power of Authenticity ................................ 92

Who Are You? ..................................................... 98

Freedom ............................................................... 113

The "Gamble" ...................................................... 123

Index ..................................................................... 135

# Forward

Ben Ellard's book, Gambling With Grace, reminds me of an experience I had when I was about three years old that changed my life. Obviously, now well in to my fifth decade of life, memories of my toddler years are vague at best, but this one, while foggy, is seared into my aging mind like grill marks on a good steak.

I had a dog but try as I might I can't remember his name anymore, I just remember him as my first dog. He was brown and white, maybe an Australian Shepherd or, more probably, a mix of thirty of forty breeds that wound up resembling an Aussy only in the tone of it's wavy coat.

My dog, who I'm certain had a name that was known to him and me, was prone to leave home for extended periods of time. I don't know if we had a hole in the fence that dad didn't fix, or maybe the dog was a digger, who knows, either way, he preferred the wide-open spaces to the confines of our little house in Fontana, California. So part of the memory I have of my little shepherd-esque dog is that he wasn't home much. Still, he accomplished something that effected my life profoundly one day when I was sitting out on the porch and he returned from one of his usual walkabout's.

He brought me a gift.

In my memory I see the little guy appear at the edge of our yard carrying something in his mouth - seeing me sitting there, he made a bee-line for the porch like reaching my chubby little smiling face signaled the completion of his journey. He made it across the yard in a few graceful strides and dropped the present in my lap. It was gooey with dog drool but I picked it up, my entire three year old being filled with elation that my old dog had brought me a gift. Something for me, especially for me. I giggled and laughed and probably wet myself although that's not part of the memory. I patted his little head and you could tell he, too, was excited to be the bearer of something that made his little pudgy human so happy.

I picked up the gift and inspected it. Now, by age three I was pretty worldly wise, especially in the area of sports, my old man having been a semi-pro catcher back in Oklahoma, so, even though I probably couldn't yet compose a complete sentence, I knew a baseball glove when I saw one. And tucked inside the glove, shoved deep in the old pocket like egg in its mothers nest, was a baseball, a dirty old thread-bare ball that had seen some real playing time in it's day.

My dog had brought me a ball and glove. I didn't gather at the time that he probably grabbed it from a local little league field between innings and had half the team chasing him for blocks to retrieve it, to me, it was his special gift to me. And it changed my life.

I became a ball player. My mom said that old glove rarely left my hand as I tossed the ball into it and pretended to be Willie Mays catching the long fly-ball to win the series. Dad capitalized on my passion and taught me to play. I played baseball all through my childhood and as a young man and it remains my favorite sport to this day. I just love it. I love everything about it.

And that love started fifty years ago when this little dog that history won't even remember with a name, brought a little boy an old mitt and ball. It was a gift I'll never forget. A gift that changed my life.

You might be holding in your hand a similar gift. The message woven through these pages is one that people in the western culture need to understand. It's the message of God's grace. When the message of grace fell into the lap of twenty-something Ben Ellard, it changed his life, his passion and his reason for living. Grace will do that. It's the grace of God poured lavishly upon mankind through the finished work of Jesus Christ. Coincidently, the word in the original bible language for grace is 'charis' which is also translated as, you guessed it, *gift*. God has a gift for you, friend, one that can change your life forever. It's His grace and He's ready to run to you and drop it in your lap. Read on and receive.

In Christ,

Edward Goble

Novelist and author of the acclaimed non-fiction book, "And No Religion, Too."

# Introduction

I became a Christian at the age of sixteen but found my sanity when I was twenty-two. When I became a Christian, I didn't go forward on a Sunday morning and recite a prayer, or fill out a questionnaire so that people knew that I understood what I was doing. In my case, my uncertainty of where I would spend eternity just caught up with me one night. I was lying in my bed on Friday night, January 29, 2002 and I cried out to Jesus to come into my life and be my Savior. A miraculous rush came over me that night, one that I could not identify at the time. All I knew was that I was no longer destined for hell, rather my final destination was now with Christ in the heavenly realms. I didn't know what that looked like at the time and I am still not sure. I became a Christian when I realized that if heaven is just a shack and if Jesus is there with me, I would be more than ecstatic with that. I was adopted by Him. He saved me.

However, this sense of liberation lasted only a short time. What I thought was going to be this incredible relationship with the Almighty God, turned out to be like an exchange of burdens; meaning, that when I decided to follow Christ, I anticipated a relationship. I thought I was going to be able to cast all my junk on Him and He would love me. What I found out is that most people in practice do not agree with that statement. The more I went to church, the more I found out how unrighteous I was, how incredibly bad I sin, and how I can never measure up. The solution? I tried to buck up, tried harder, and did my best to sell out for Him. I had exchanged my burden of sin for a whole new set of burdens; the Law. I thought the only way I could experience the relationship I felt that night in my room would be to make Him pleased with me.

I had a solid high school career where I graduated in the top 10% of my class, received a wrestling scholarship, made it to the state golf tournament, and had a good support system of friends and family. I turned down a wrestling scholarship to Campbellsville University in the summer of 2004 and chose to follow in my parents footsteps at Oklahoma Baptist University along with several of my friends. It was here when things started to get dicey. My friends made new friends and I became a distant memory. I was living in the dormitory on campus. I was surrounded by 2,000 people on any given day, yet never had I felt more alone. I wasn't into the party scene, yet I wasn't walking around with my Bible under my arm either. I was in this gray area of labels. I didn't fit in. No matter how hard I tried, I couldn't feel comfortable. I began to wear a mask with an aura of "everything's fine" while adding a smile for good measure. Underneath the facade, I was broken, sad, depressed, worn out, and tired.

Alcohol became the only thing to get me through the day and in my mind at least, it was dependable.

One drink led to another and another. Before I knew it I was drinking every day, not caring about my grades, people, including my parents. Professors started to see a decline in my preparation and studies. I remember going to a New Testament class in a drunken stupor trying to figure out how I could have been so close to God, yet, now felt so far away. Instead of seeking help, I went back to my dorm, and opened up another beer - and down the hatch. I suppose that certain addicts need to hit rock bottom before they can look up. My rock bottom hit March 25th while lying on my loft half drunk.

I badly wanted to stop drinking knowing it would kill me if I did not seek help. I tested God that night. I said "What the hell am I doing? Why am I like this? God, if You still care about me at all, even a little sliver, then why don't You do something? I don't want this, I don't want to want it. If You're there, please just make me stop." And He did.

On March 26th I became sober. A week later I received an email from Campbellsville University recruiting me again to be on their wrestling roster. I gladly accepted their offer and made the trip to Campbellsville, Kentucky the following fall semester where I was introduced to some incredible people, people I now consider family. However, my spiritual life was still loaded down with rules, ought, and shame. I would beat myself up spiritually if I happened to "miss the mark". I thought it was honorable to feel bad when you mess up. I was miserable and at my wits end.

In September of 2008, I went to Fishers, Indiana, to hang out with a family friend, Rusty Kennedy. We went to a football game, which I do not remember, where Rusty sensed the motivation to tell me about how I can live free-free to live out of who God says I am, and he unpacked this thing called grace. He laid it out there like a buffet of glorious food. It was like hearing the Gospel for the very first time. The message of grace was liberating and has since completely changed my perspective of life.

From that September night, I began to understand the good news of the Gospel. I realized that His grace is enough and my behavior does not dictate who I am, but my new birth in Christ does. I started to understand that there has only been one person that had perfect behavior and it is by His grace that I can desire purity. Soon, I discovered that this perspective enables me to live the free abundant life He offers.

Rusty has been an incredible influence in my life and I am thankful for his sensitivity to the Holy Spirit and tenderness with my fragile heart. I am finally comfortable to "live out of who God says I am", so let the journey begin…

# 1

# The Cross

Dear Friend,

    While backpacking in the mountains and canyons of northern Alabama, I was listening to Bruce Springsteen's "Jungleland" and Gov't Mule's "Soulshine". Those two songs are always on my playlist when I find myself surrounded by God's great scenery. As I was listening and praying, God gave me a sense of a revelation. So I walked more, prayed more, and listened to where He was leading my thoughts. As my thoughts turned, I was brought to this statement, *"I believe an understanding of the cross will make sinners run to it, and if saints fully understood it, they would live differently."*

The more I studied the Word of God, the more I learned that the thirty-three years of Christ's life revolutionized the world. Yet, one event radically changed how we can live today.

It goes all the way back to Genesis. Adam sinned and the result is that we are now born with a sin nature. Some may be upset that Adam caused us to inherit sin. I know I was for the longest time. I hated the fact that because he screwed up, I now am messed up from my first breath. Perhaps an appropriate analogy would go something like this: in football, when someone messes up, it's not just that specific individual that gets penalized, it's the entire team. If someone jumps off sides, then that person is not penalized five yards, the whole team is. All of mankind has been placed on Adam's team, and we are penalized as a result. Consequently, we have inherited a sin nature.

Sin has a wage – its payment is death. Romans 6:23

says, *"for the wages of sin is death"*. Jesus also mentions it in the Lord's Prayer, *"forgive us our debts"* [1]. Through our mishaps, we have acquired some pretty hefty debt. Unfortunately, no one can pay for sin and live, because we're all in debt. One thing that the Law shows is how much "debt" we have.

Here is the dilemma. Sin separates us from the relationship with God. The price of this sin, the removal of the stain, is death. Yet, the kicker is that the person getting us out of debt cannot be in debt themselves. God decided that He would send His Son, in the form of a man. Jesus is a man without fault. Could He be the sacrifice we have been yearning for and needing for so long? The Bible says;

*"But He was wounded for our transgressions, He was bruised for our iniquities; the chastisement for our peace was upon Him, and by His stripes we are healed." - Isaiah 53:5*

As Jesus hung on the cross, He was offered myrrh, a painkiller mixed with sour wine. Yet He was unwilling to drink. I find it liberating that He would do such a thing. He refused to drink the painkiller and face every ounce of pain - authentic, physical and spiritual pain so we never would have to in the way He did. Amazing, isn't it, that even when He was dying, suffering, in excruciating pain, He was thinking about you.

Why did Jesus go through this? He did so that we could become the righteousness of God in Him by faith. So that He could reside in those that say "yes" to the finished work of the cross. He did this so He may transform our hearts in such a way that it's possible to eliminate the sin nature that once bound us to sin. We didn't break even on this deal. God's grace super abounds. Sin may be a wildfire, but God's grace is a massive amount of water than can extinguish the flames in one remarkable instant.

Live Free, Rest Easy,

Ben.

# 2

# The Beauty of Covenant

Dear Friend,

In previous years, when I read the Bible, I would be overwhelmed. In order to not feel that confusion, I chose to not pay attention to what the Bible had to say about my life. I was blinded to the personal meaning. The Bible talks about covenants and I had no understanding what that word even meant. As I felt the Lord leading me to open what I saw as the intimidating book I learned some beautiful life changing truths through understanding covenant. There are multiple covenants the Bible mentions, but I do not want my letter to you to be one of theological academia. Rather, I want to share with you a liberating truth.

A covenant is a deep-rooted commitment between two parties. Different from a contract, a covenant is to establish relationship, not a business venture. Malcolm Smith's book <u>The Power of the Blood Covenant</u> uses this definition of covenant:

*"A covenant is a binding, unbreakable obligation between two parties, based on unconditional love sealed by blood and sacred oath, that creates a relationship in which each party is bound by specific undertakings on each other's behalf. The parties to the covenant place themselves under the penalty of divine retribution should they later attempt to avoid those undertakings."* [1]

The first time that you see a covenant being made between God and man is in Genesis 15. God promised Abraham that he would inherit the land of Ur (Genesis 15:7). Abraham asked God how he was going to possess it and this is where we find the first physical manifestation of covenant. God told Abraham to bring Him a three year old heifer, a three year old female goat, a three year old ram, a turtledove, and a young pigeon, all representing the socioeconomic classes of that day; from richest (heifer) to poorest (young pigeon). I love this correlation because it symbolizes that no matter how much money you have or how little money you have, God is for you.

In essence, God made a covenant with His Son that Abraham would be a father of many nations and that he would inherit a great amount of land (Genesis 15:5, 18). Later, this promise comes to pass.

Jewish tradition states the blood that is caught during the division of the animals would be sprinkled where there was a walking pathway between the bodies of the animals. One person would stand on one side of the bodies while the other would stand at the opposite end. Each person would cut their wrists or arms so their blood would be shed as well and they would walk to the center of the dead animals. They would, at that point, clasp their hands together signifying a union, and then release their grip and walk past one another to where the other person stood at the beginning of the ceremony. When each person had arrived at their respective places, they would turn around and face one another signifying that they have entered into covenant. The scars they would possess on their arms served as constant reminders that they were in covenant with someone. Blood had to flow to seal the covenant between two partners, because *"the life of the flesh is in the blood"* (Leviticus 17:11). Since blood was shed to get into covenant, blood would also have to be shed to get out of it. In other words, if you didn't think you could keep the covenant; reject the proposition of entering it.

There are two primary covenants the Scripture speaks on; the Old Covenant and the New Covenant. The two are distinctively different in multiple ways. In the Old Covenant, God gave man something incredibly holy, and righteous for them to use; the Law. God cut a pure and just covenant. When He gave the Law (i.e. the Ten Commandments and the written laws), it exposed the righteousness of God, the character of God and the separation God has with a dark world.

There was nothing wrong with God initiating the Old Covenant. God gave something perfect to people who were imperfect; and here rests a problem. Imperfection is incapable of achieving perfection on its own. So, why then did God give something perfect to a group of people that were imperfect? This question used to eat away at my heart because it seemed as if God was different before than He is today. My head would go crazy trying to wrap my mind around this concept of God being the same, yet seeing the path of destruction in the Old Testament. As I prayed one night, I felt the Holy Spirit say "Son, God did not give people the Law so that He would show off how righteous He is; rather He gave the Law to show an unholy world how unholy they are." After God gave the Law in Exodus, the people said "All the words which the LORD has spoken we will do!" (Exodus 24:3) and at that point, Moses sprinkled them with the blood of the covenant.

I have some atheistic friends that suggest to me "I

would rather burn in hell than to worship a God that punishes people and torments people if they don't obey every word He says." In previous years, I started to see where they were coming from. But now, as I have read the Bible and learned the character of God in the context of covenants, I have realized that God didn't punish the people because he hated them, but He was merely honoring covenant. He hasn't changed, nor will He ever change. After all, the reason why punishment occurred at that time was because God was honoring the specificities of the covenant He and the people of Israel agreed upon.

Mount Sinai is where God gave the people the Law for their safety and profit. However, this covenant was conditional. If the people would obey *all* the laws, then God would bless them and they would be His special treasure (Exodus 19:5) - if they did not obey them, they would be cursed.

Since the Law was perfect, it demanded perfection. No one could live up to the bar set by the Law since they were imperfect by nature. It was given to be their tutor to drive them to see their need for justification by faith since they were incapable of living such a perfect life. That's love –tough love.

Within the context of the Old Covenant, forgiveness had pro's and cons. Once a year, on the Day of Atonement, the High Priest would sprinkle blood of a bull on the mercy seat of the Ark of the Covenant in order to cover the sins the people committed during that year. However, the bad news to this situation is that the next day, a person's sins started to acquire and add up again. As a result, sacrifices were required year after year. In doing so, God gave the people an opportunity to experience relief from the guilt of their sins. It is important to remember that the sacrifices were incapable of taking away sins-they could only cover them. People could experience God's forgiveness, but within the context of the Old Covenant, there was no final solution. For this reason, the Law is only a shadow of things to come. It stands as a picture of the finished work Christ completed on the cross in His sacrificial death- not a reality for those under the Old Covenant.

There have been sermons preached that God gave the Ten Commandments because He wanted to expose His holiness. But please realize God didn't give people the Ten Commandments to show how holy He is. No one's mind can wrap around God's holiness through two stone tablets. Along with the original Ten Commandments, there were 613 laws given by God Himself through man's pen in the books of Exodus and Leviticus. If God was to use the law to show people how holy He was it would make sense then, to say that He would be holier if there were 614 laws.

The Law was not given to motivate man to jump up to a proverbial bar that was set above their heads. It was given to show mankind their inability to jump at all. God built something that was too high for us to attain. Did God make a mistake? Absolutely not! The Law is righteous, holy, and just - which is a picture of who God is. He set the Law where He did so those trying to live up to the bar would be completely exhausted at their attempts at trying to buck up and be better and find themselves finally laying at the foot of the cross saying "ok, I claim Jesus." Jesus, when He came, did not come to abolish the Law, but to fulfill it. He lived it perfectly. Then, when on the cross, He became our perfect sacrifice.

Many people put themselves in a confusing cycle of condemnation and shame when they try to apply an Old Covenant, law-based mentality to understanding the Bible. I have been witness to many people trying to apply the Sermon on the Mount to their lives. What results is an instantaneous feeling of guilt, shame and condemnation. Immediately they try to cleanse themselves of all "unrighteousness" and then subject themselves to the very laws they are incapable of keeping. Jesus intensified the Law to establish that those attempting to be justified by the Law fail miserably, even on their best day. He said things like, *"but I say to you that everyone who looks at a woman with lust for her has already committed adultery with her in his heart. If your right eye makes you stumble, tear it out and throw it from you; if your right hand makes you stumble, cut it off and throw it from you."* - Matthew 5:28-30.

A pastor once said to me "it is clear Jesus didn't *really* mean those things." However, if you come to the conclusion that we are supposed to do everything Jesus said, then there is no room for picking and choosing. The fact is that if we don't read the Scripture in the context of the covenants, we will end up manipulating the perfect, inerrant Word of God. That's no way to utilize the Scripture; especially if the good news is exclaimed in the book.

What can be concluded from the Sermon on the Mount is that you cannot do it on your own. The Sermon on the Mount and the Beatitudes should not be our goal. Walking by the Spirit and allowing Him to work through us is the goal and calling for every believer - staying focused on Jesus. Do not think that I am saying Jesus' words are unimportant or not inspired by God. I believe His words *are* important and relevant- however they need to be appropriated to the correct context and audience.

Given that no one could live up to the provisions of the Law, everyone experienced fear, guilt, and shame.

As a result, they could never draw near to God. The Old Covenant left people condemned and in need of something better and new. Hebrews says:

"The former regulation is set aside because it was weak and useless (for the law made nothing perfect), and a better hope is introduced, by which we draw near to God." - Hebrews 7:18-19.

Since the New Covenant has come, we have obtained our perfect sacrifice – Jesus. He died for all sin, once for all time. [2]

Where the Old Covenant signifies the giving of the Law and animal sacrifices for forgiveness of sins; the New Covenant is ushered in by the death of Christ - the world's sufficient sacrifice. It is important to keep in mind that the New Covenant doesn't start with the first words of the New Testament. *The New Covenant starts at the death of Jesus.* This is vital because it will relieve much confusion when you begin to read the Bible.

The new covenant ushered in grace whereby the dividing line that separated the Jews and the Gentiles was abolished and unity by faith took its place.

Grace - it's something that you don't deserve, that you'll never have to pay for. Grace is not just forgiving you of the sins of your past, but future as well. Grace is not just a ticket that will get you into heaven, but grace is also the ability of Him in you to do His will on a daily basis while you're here on earth. Grace is not something that you can manipulate for evil, but it is the replacement of the "old you" and puts a new heart in you, for you, to live an abundant life through you.

2 Corinthians 5:21 says that Jesus was *"made to be sin"* in order that He might die. It says that He was made to be sin signifying that He was not dying for His sin because He was sinful, but that He may be the perfect sacrifice for our sins. Let's take a look at the implications of the cross. Darkness fell over the earth for three hours, the day Christ died. I read about the crucifixion shortly after I read about the covenants and what they meant. I came to this conclusion with the help of the Holy Spirit; God's back was to Jesus when He looked up and said "My God, My God, why have

You forsaken Me?"[3] The reason God's back was facing His Son is because God and Jesus were initiating a new covenant. Remember when two people would walk past each other to get to the other side of the dead animals, after having met in the middle and clasped hands, they would walk with their backs to each other until they made it to the other side, at which point they would turn around. It was black because God's back was to Jesus as they were initiating the new covenant. When it became light again on the earth, and the Father and Son face each other signifying that they have entered into another covenant, Jesus says "Father, into Your hands, I commit My Spirit."

When Jesus Christ died, He exchanged His place for yours. The curse that was on us because we could not keep the Law was taken upon Jesus Himself on the cross. Then something incredible happened. Jesus Christ, who had taken the curse for us, replaced the Law for grace. Grace, where the enmity that once separated the Jews and Gentiles was abolished and erased through His sacrificial death.[4] That's why Paul writes in Romans 6:14 *"you are no longer under law, but under grace."* Jesus took the curse, He's the only one who had the right to take the law and throw it out of the way and replace it with grace, goodness, mercy, and forgiveness for everyone. As a result of the finished work of Christ, you no longer have to jump to reach the bar of the law, you just have to stand there and let Him pour His sufficient grace upon you. Where the Law pushed you down with condemnation and death, how much more glorious is the ministry of grace and righteousness where you just have to stand at the foot of the cross and let Him pour His strength, Power, Love, and Life in you- something that Old Covenant believers never got to experience. The Old Covenant says "I will by no means wipe clean the slate of the guilty". The New Covenant says "I will by no means hold anything against My people [those that believe Him by faith]". If God were to expose His wrath on to you right now, then Jesus lied when hanging on the cross as He said "it is finished". Are you beginning to recognize the importance of appropriating the Old Covenant and the New Covenant?

Love you, Rest easy,

Ben

# 3

# Loving to Death

Dear Friend,

Jesus said, *"If you keep My commandments, you will abide in My love; just as I have kept My Father's commandments and abide in His love. These things I have spoken to you so that My joy may be in you, and that your joy may be made full. This is My commandment, that you love one another, just as I have loved you."* - John 15:10-12

There is a difference between this and what was mentioned in Matthew 22. Remember, the question the religious asked Jesus "Hey Master, what is the greatest commandment *in the Law*?" [1]  Jesus responded by saying "You want the Law's greatest commandment? Love the Lord your God with all your heart, soul, mind and strength and love your neighbor as yourself." That's the best the Law can do. But He gives us a new commandment that is appropriated with the covenant to come; the new covenant of grace. He says "Love your neighbor as I have loved you." People might ask "How is that a new commandment?"  Notice where the emphasis lies. It is not on your ability to love your neighbor, but rather it is on Him loving you. You can't know how to love under the new commandment unless you realize how loved you are. If you have no knowledge of how loved you are, it is impossible to know how to love your neighbor. Jesus goes on to say that "Greater love has no one than this, that one lay down his life for his friends." Growing up in church, this verse was tweaked into saying "greater love has no one than this, that one lay down his life for his friends. Would you die for your friends? You're supposed to love people that much." This new commandment was turned into being a law based, guilt ridden attempt at loving those around me. There was no way I could have loved my friends enough to die for them. I was eight years old. I had too much of a sporting career for my life to end because I died for a little snotty punk that stole my lunch money.

Fast forward and I am now twenty five years old and find it equally challenging to die for a stranger. I think we can all honestly admit that it's too difficult to love your neighbor as yourself. You love yourself more than you love your neighbor. For example, during the holidays your family takes a family photo. Who's the first person you look at? Yourself, right? The satisfaction of the photograph is contingent on how well you look. Everyone else could be looking like they just got out of the van with Cheech and Chong and as long as your eyes aren't closed and you're smiling the best smile you can possibly muster up; then the photograph is considered, by you, a quality picture. With that said, how in the world can we fulfill this commandment of loving our neighbors as He has loved us? The commandment has nothing to do with your effort. It has everything to do with showing you how much you're loved. No one had ever seen the amount of love one could have by dying for someone else. Jesus died for you. The day you start getting that revelation in your life, loving your neighbor becomes easier.

We cannot understand what love is if we are only told about it over and over again. Even if the mountains move and the trees clap, and the oceans roar, that still does not display love for us. Those are impersonal byproducts of His love. But, you get an idea of what love is when you see your sins in His body and His body being broken and judged on your behalf so that you may be made the righteousness of God in Christ.

*"For I determined to know nothing among you except Jesus Christ, and Him crucified."* 1 Corinthians 2:2

*"We know love by this, that He laid down His life for us; and we ought to lay down our lives for the brethren."*- 1 John 3:16

*"Greater love has no one than this, that one lay*

*down his life for his friends."* - John 15:13

*"But God demonstrates His own love toward us, in that while we were yet sinners, Christ died for us."* - *Romans 5:8*

Perhaps the crucifixion shows the depth of love Christ has for us. This love displayed on the cross is personal, true, and real. When we truly look at the cross, we see love manifested. Love that yet while we were sinners, Christ died for us (Romans 5:8). This is a love that has no secret agenda, no trapdoor, no lists of violations or offenses; a love that does not require anything, it simply is. He did not die because we were saints, but when we were sinners! 1 Corinthians 2:2 is a verse that resonates within my soul. I believe the Spirit has revealed to me that this death is manifested love. Check out what road we're on now - love. What are the benefits of knowing His love? Freedom. Peace. Patience. Joy. Happiness. Gentleness. Comfort. Protection. Safety. Authenticity. No condemnation. No guilt. No shame. Righteousness. Life. Grace. Mercy. New nature. New identity. New spirit.

Forgiveness is liberating. Yet, the cross of Christ provided that and more. We now have the strength and ability to conquer what once held us in bondage. His love demonstrated on the cross ignites this incredible gift. Evil was defeated and we can now and forever live from the point of victory. The finished work of Christ is here. The only requirement is faith in Him. It's no wonder why Paul stated "For I have determined to know nothing among you except Christ and Him crucified"[2]. I have determined to know nothing but Christ and His love that transforms lives. It did mine.

Live Free. Rest Easy,

Ben

# 4

# Sufficient Forgiveness

Dear Friend,

I have asked people how often they ask God to forgive them and the answer I almost always get is "every day". About five years ago, I would have given you the same answer. Every night before I went go to bed, I would pray that He would forgive me of my sins. I thought that that prayer would suffice until the morning and before I would eat breakfast, I would have to recite that prayer again to make sure I was covered. The more I would say that prayer, the more I couldn't help but think I was a disappointment to God. I thought of myself as a defeated, lowly sinner. But because of that prayer, He had to accept me. My view of God had become skewed and I thought it was as if He had accepted me because He had to.

A few months after that September night with Rusty, I found myself reading in bed one night trying to make myself fall asleep. Then something remarkable was revealed to me. It came in the form of a hypothetical situation. Let's say you wake up every morning and ask your father to be your father. Every night before you go to bed, you ask your father to be your father. I believe that after just a few times of this occurring, your father might sit you down and tell you in perhaps a stern voice "No matter what you do, you're my child. I will never not be your father." This is analogous with the way Christ views those asking Him to forgive them day after day. God is not limited to time or space. He has a bird's eye view over your life and when you ask Him initially to forgive you of your sins, He does not just merely see the *past* sins, but He's aware of the present and future sins you will commit as well; and He erases them.

Growing up, I was told that if you sin, it's the same as nailing Jesus to the cross. So, instantly you are brought under law. This is how I lived for the first six years of my faith. I was obsessive compulsive with my relationship with Him. Although the motive may in some ways be good, the theology and application is unbiblical. Ephesians 4:32 says, *"Be kind to one another, tender-hearted, forgiving each other, just as God in Christ also has forgiven you"*. Are you tracking with me? Christ's forgiveness is past tense and sufficient forever. Christ died to forgive all sins. Asking Him to forgive you is the same as asking Him to die again.

*"AND THEIR SINS AND THEIR LAWLESS DEEDS I WILL REMEMBER NO MORE." Now where there is forgiveness of these things, there is no longer any offering for sin."* - Hebrews 10:17-18

In other words, Christ died for your sins; to erase them and separate them as far as the east is from the west (Psalm 103:12).

I am convinced that looking at life through this lens

will enable you to see clearly the truth about how much He so desperately wants you.[1] What I am saying in relation to God's forgiveness is that you never again have to ask for it; for you already possess it! Be thankful for it like you were when you received that bike under the Christmas tree! It is yours. Whew, what a night that was! I'll never forget it. All I wanted to do the next day is get on my one speed cruiser bike and go tell people about this incredible truth I realized the previous night. There are those that will resist believing such a notion. They'll hang on to their belief that it's up to them to ask for this release of sins day in and day out. I've had conversations with people that say "Well, its really just semantics. I say please forgive me as a humble reminder of what He's done." Friend, this is not just a semantic technicality. I have hardly ever heard someone pray and give thanks that Christ's blood is sufficient for their forgiveness. On the contrary, I've heard more people asking for His forgiveness as if their previous sin was not erased at their conversion. Sins are not merely covered like dust under the rug; but, they are completely erased.[2] Christ's blood is a sufficient eraser, not a blanket. The sins of those who believe in Him are erased, remembered by Him no more. They are separated from us as far as the East is from the West.[3]

The Holy Spirit, through the grace of God has given us a new identity; a new heart.[4] Our new identity, as we grow and mature, no longer desires the old sinful lusts of our past, rather it's desire is righteousness. After all, Romans 6:23 says that the "wages of sin is death", so why in the world would Paul be preaching a gospel that freely allows people to commit spiritual suicide? The Gospel is about Life, not death.[5]

If God loved you so much that He would willingly lay down His life for you while you were a sinner, how greater do you think His love is for you now that you're the righteousness of God in Christ? You may wonder about your past and all the mistakes you've made. Friend, it's not what you've done that determines who you are. It's about knowing who you are in Christ. Are you struggling with addiction, lust, foul mouth, gossip, or bad thoughts? Instead of focusing on your failures, I invite you to focus on the righteousness of God in

Christ in you.  You are who He says you are.  This is not a game of pop psychology, a mind game, or any attempt to make you feel good even though you're an evil, vile person.  Faith comes by hearing and hearing comes by the Word of God.[6]  Unfortunately, when you don't walk in faith, you walk by sight; and when you walk by sight, you hear man's speaking, not God's.  I encourage you to not accept what the world has to offer you, but what Christ, through faith can offer you; a new life with better promises.

Since sins could never be paid for by the animal sacrifices under the Old Covenant, there had to be a sacrifice without any blemish.  Christ came into the world for this very reason.  He offered His body as a spotless sacrifice and led to the New Covenant.  The degree by which we are forgiven is best represented in a past action, completed action, with a resulting state of being.  In other words, it's been done and will never be reversed.  Consequently, God remembers our sins no more.[7] Jesus has done it all.

There are two natural reactions we have as believers

when we commit an act of sin – confess and repent. We do so never to gain forgiveness however. The reason for these two actions is to "clear out the static in the phone line" so the voice of God is being heard more clearly. Confession ("to agree with") and repentance ("changing one's mind") are vital in how a believer must deal with sin. You see, the difference between the repentance of a non-believer and the repentance of a believer is that repentance for a non believer results in forgiveness, whereas a believer's repentance results in restoring fellowship with God. Our love for Christ then becomes the motivation to act, not duty or law.

Live Free, Rest Easy,
Ben

# 5

# The Heart of Love

Dear Friend,

I decided to have some late night coffee, listen to Jesus, and worship. So, I found myself at a local restaurant, just me and Jesus, surrounded by people who probably thought I was dining alone. I think about God's forgiveness of *all* my sins forever; and I think "*Wow*, that's unexplainable outside of the love of Christ." His love for me is indescribable, that even in my deepest abyss, His grace reaches down and pulls me out every time. If it all ended there, our freedom, experience, and relationship with Him would be greater than a lifetime supply of gummy bears. Perhaps the most incredible truth of this Gospel is the fact that He has put His nature, power, and love inside of us at our disposal! While sitting in the lonely restaurant tonight with a cup of coffee in my hands, He reiterates this message, "I love you, and you've been forgiven. My child, you *are* the righteousness of God in Me. You've got My Spirit, love, and power. You have all of Me." I am my Beloved's and He is mine! Amazing!

I've seen in many churches where the pastor loves his "flock" in general, but doesn't or can't really know each of them on a personal level. In the same way, I think it's easy for us to see Christ on the cross as He died for the world. He loves everyone He died for, but to think He could have a personal relationship with each of them, seems out of the realm of possibility. This is where my Jesus rocks my socks clean off. He is persistent in wooing me back to Him even when I experience those days where I neglect Him. He loves me anyway.

He *loves* me. Ben Ellard; the guy with tattoos, a chest long goatee, and living in a remote town in the middle of Kentucky. *That* guy. He loves *me*. Not only does God love me, but He loves me to the very extent that He loves His Son. The beauty of this incredible love is that it's not reserved for me, dear friend. This love, the same exact love that God loves His one and only Son with, is reserved for you, even on your worst day. For the past couple weeks my Spirit has rested in the same manner as it did when I first met Him, in the person of Jesus. It is my hope and prayer that this experience, that is personal to me, will become personal to you as well.

When asked by the disciples "how should we pray?" Jesus answered them by saying *"Our Father"*. This had to blow the minds of the disciples. I can only imagine hearing for the first time "Father" referencing "God". Up until that point, God was a distant entity; but when Christ came, He was Father. Based on Romans 8:15, we have the right to call Him *"Abba, Father"*. Romans 8:15 says, *"For you did not receive the spirit of bondage again to fear, but you received the Spirit of adoption by whom we cry out, "Abba, Father."* What is so unique and special about this now is that the word "Abba" softens the word after it. For example, in the context of "Abba, Father", it is translated to "Daddy". When we refer to Him as "Daddy" we are referencing every emotion that is attached to Him.

If you have trouble with the fact that you can call Him "Daddy" because, in your eyes, He is an Almighty, formal God, then I encourage you to realize that you are now a recipient of amazing promises; that you are no longer under law, but under grace. With those two things being true, it only stands to reason that God is tired of the distance, and ready for a relationship; a close love relationship.

Live Free, Rest Easy,

Ben

# 6

# The Gift of No Condemnation

Dear Friend,

As a child of God, it is imperative to remember two important words – no condemnation. Jesus does not ever want to remind you where you were. You, my friend, are a child of the living God. If you find yourself in the hog pins of life, remembering who you are will bring you to your senses and you'll naturally find yourself walking back to the Father. When you return, He will remind you of who you are.

During my early years of trying to figure out how to live this Christian life, I honestly didn't have a clue. I didn't know what it was supposed to look like. I thought more effort would make Him pleased with me, but at the same time, I was starting to feel the shackles wrap tighter around my wrists. My life was a prison of rules and doing the right thing and feeling like scum for doing the bad. I felt so ashamed. I thought God had turned His back on me when I sinned, when I failed to hit the mark. I wanted God to be on my side, but I didn't feel like I appreciated what He did for me enough for that to happen.

I was putting myself under a lot of pressure. I'm incapable of living up to every expectation people place on me (and I'd be willing to bet you are too). I soon found out that Christianity is first and foremost *not* a religion; rather it is an identity.[1] For me to say that God condemns me when I sin is not only unbiblical,[2] but that mindset also makes Jesus Christ and His work on the cross insufficient. If Christ is our Savior, how can we continue to be condemned? Did God condemn sin?

ABSOLUTELY! He turned His back on His only Son and judged sin through His Son so that we would not have to face such punishment.[3] Christ took the sins of the world and paid the price so that we would not have to. He exchanged His life for ours.

Unfortunately, I have witnessed many well intentioned people try to earn something that has already been paid for, specifically salvation through faith in Jesus. Jesus died one time, once for all.[4] It is up to us to accept this sufficient gift of salvation. If that sufficiency is rejected, we try to do better, relying on our self effort to bring us closer to God so we may appear more presentable. Jesus loves you, desires you, and wants you.

If you're in that place where you find yourself trying to look better to gain the acceptance of God, I implore you to look at His followers. One was a tax collector whose reputation was as a thief. However, he repented immediately when approached by Jesus and began to preach the Gospel of Christ. Another was a prostitute who became a follower of Him and was among the first to share about Jesus' resurrection. Still, another man was persecuting the church. Paul empowered the persecution and destruction of the Church. However, Paul soon turned to Christ and began teaching and serving the very people he had tried to stop.

None of these people I mentioned tried to do better to look good so that God would show favor on them. Instead, they came to Christ with all of their sins and trusted God. My encouragement, dear friend, is to focus on Christ, and allow Him to take care of your issues. I encourage you to fix your eyes on Him. I pray that the Spirit will show you that He's not mad at you for the things you may have done in the past. With Jesus, condemnation ceases to exist.

Much love,
Ben

# 7

# Jesus

Dear Friend,

I'm overwhelmed yet again at how lovely Jesus is. So much so, that I feel it burning in my heart to just tell someone about it. It appears you've received the winning ticket. I was out late last night listening, praying, and talking to Jesus, when I broke down and tears filled my eyes. They weren't tears of sadness, depression, or because I was just bummed out. The tears were a result of my remembrance of just how lovely Jesus is. I'm not here to talk about other churches, or their messages, because frankly, I don't know exactly what they preach. However, I do have some dear friends of mine that no longer fellowship with other believers. They have felt jaded, resented, and judged. Their words to me consisted of hell fire and damnation. Steve-O, a famous actor from the movie Jackass once told Tom Greene "What happened to being good, to feel good, for being good; instead of being good because you're afraid of hell? Intimidation and organized religion can [explicit language]. I do not hate Jesus but I passionately hate the crimes committed against humanity in the name of Jesus." I could not agree more with that statement. I think Steve-O and I, in part, share some common thread in this arena. Unfortunately a good portion of messages that get presented from mainstream churches is that Jesus is sitting on His throne ready to smite, curse, and punish those He either does not like, or that He just feels like should be punished. Such intimidation does not reconcile us to Him. In fact, most would run away from such horror. It's like Jesus is the bully of the playground and no one wants to swing freely from the proverbial monkey bars anymore.

I want to tell you about how lovely my Jesus is. It is my hope, sincere hope that Jesus is presented to you as more lovely than dangerously vengeful as it is who He truly is. Jesus is lovely because He is the light that shines in the midst of the darkness. Jesus is lovely because He is the sacrifice for your sins. Jesus is lovely because He brought you grace instead of making you come and get it. Jesus is lovely because He takes the ordinary and makes it extraordinary. He is the manifestation for the phrase "for God so loved the world". He is lovely because He steps into your life when you're at your most embarrassed, ashamed, and humiliated part of your life; and even when the rest of the world tells you that you're not worth it, He makes you the center of His attention. He takes all the things that you can't do and injects His Spirit and Life into them. He ignores what you can't do, and helps those that can't help themselves. He always remembers the most important thing about who you are is not about where you live or what you've done; but it's whether or not you know that His body was broken for you and His blood was spilled for you. Jesus is lovely because no matter how much junk you bring to the table, His response is "neither do I condemn you" (John 8:11).

You don't have to know theology or doctrine or go to seminary; but one thing is certain, you "see" when you meet Him. Jesus is lovely because He sets you free from sin, guilt, and condemnation even before He sets you free from all the junk you've been carrying around for the past weeks, months, years - perhaps even decades. He's exclusive. He presents Himself as the door and no one can come to the Father except through Him. He says you can have life and have it abundantly. He's not talking about later when you get to heaven, or sometime down the road. It's right now. Jesus is lovely because He hurts when you hurt, cries when you cry, weeps when you weep, grieves when you grieve, feels when you feel. He endured what we could never endure so that we would never have to endure it; that is, the physical pain of the cross and the spiritual agony when He looked up to His Father and said "My God, my God, why have you forsaken Me?".

The world will give you peace only after you have

paid for it; but Jesus gives you peace only after He paid for it. When He ascended to heaven, He didn't abandon nor neglect us. He sent a Helper in the form of His Spirit to reside in us. Jesus is lovely because He adopts us when we may not even feel worthy of adoption. He is the ultimate forgiver, sustainer of life. He discharges the debtors. He sets the captives free. He defends the weak and feeble. He is the Life. He is the Way. He is the very essence of Truth. He is love. He is the comforter to the broken. He's a rebel to the religious. His life fulfilled the law, and His death abolished it. He is the realization of grace and truth. He is the connection between us and God.

You can't live without Him, but you can live abundantly through Him. He's the chain breaker, the freedom giver, the grace giver, the life giver, the sacrifice. He is the alpha and omega, the Prince of Peace, Wonderful Counselor, and Mighty God. He is the beginning and the end. He is constantly wooing you with His patience, lovingkindness, and tolerance. He is the joy in our hearts. He is the Savior of the world. Death couldn't control Him and the grave couldn't keep Him still. He is the friend of sinners the Father of those who believe. He grants us blessing, life, and grace.

In the gospel of John, John writes this to finish his account of being with Jesus when he writes:

*"And there are also many other things which Jesus did, which if they were written in detail, I suppose that even the world itself would not contain the books that would be written."* - John 21:25

The only way to know how lovely, loving, and love-ridden He is is to get to know Him intimately. Knowing Him changes everything. Grace becomes vibrant. Redemption becomes personal. Mercy has a pulse. Forgiveness creates a "before and after" in the life of those who realize what took place the moment they put their trust in Jesus. There's an inheritance reserved for you to explore. How is it accessed? Jesus said it beautifully: *"Come, follow Me."*

With much love,

Ben

# 8

# Function of the Holy Spirit

Dear Friend,

The prodigal son is perhaps one of the most popular parables that Jesus ever spoke. The story goes like this: there was a son who decided that he wanted all of his inheritance from his father while his father was still alive. As soon as the father gave his son his inheritance, the son squandered it. By today's standards, the son went to Las Vegas and gambled, engaged in drunkenness, hired prostitutes, and lived a very expensive, sinful life. When the famine came and stretched over the land, the son decided to work on a farm. The Bible indicates how starved he was by stating, "And he would have gladly filled his stomach with the pods that the swine were eating, and no one was giving *anything* to him." (Luke 15:16, emphasis added). The son soon came to his senses and made the trek back home. His father, seeing his son in the distance, had tears in his eyes as he ran to his son and hugged him and kissed him.

I will pause this story for a moment and try to paint a picture of this scene for you. The son had squandered all of his money, and was now poor. It is unclear if he was able to bathe at his last employment while feeding the hogs. My guess is that he did not have such luxury. In the parable it states that the son was in a distant country. I, myself, am a recreational hiker and know the kind of stench that overwhelms my body after a long journey in the sun. Not only did this man hike in the heat, but had no shower and probably reeked of hog. None of that stood in the way of the father meeting his son and embracing him.

The son, full of remorse asks his father if he could become one of his hired hands. The father refused to even consider the notion. Before the son could finish what he was saying, his father clothed him with a robe, killed a fattened calf, and began to celebrate his son's coming home. However, his older brother was astonished and speechless at the event that had taken place. Why would the father welcome him back into his home with such trust and joy? Why wouldn't the father hire his son as a hired hand? Because there was no condemnation. The parable ends with the father addressing the older brother by saying, "And he said to him, 'Son, you have always been with me, and all that is mine is yours. But we had to celebrate and rejoice, for this brother of yours was dead and *has begun* to live, and *was* lost and has been found.'" (Luke 15:31-32, emphasis added). The dad refused to remind his son where he had been in the hog pin. I think all of us, at one time or another, will find ourselves in the hog pins of sin. But this story that Jesus tells is so beautiful as it relates Him with us.

It is my encouragement that when we find ourselves

in the hog pin, that we "come to our senses" and go back to our Father. Upon our return, you won't have to worry about whether or not your Heavenly Father will see you as dirty, filthy, or grungy. Instead, He will greet you, wash you off and remind you of who you are, not what you did. *That* is my Father. Do you know Him?

*"For God did not send His Son into the world to condemn the world, but that the world through Him might be saved.* - John 3:17

*For the Law was given through Moses; grace and truth were realized through Jesus Christ.* - John 1:17

*"Do not think that I will accuse you before the Father; the one who accuses you is Moses, in whom you have set your hope.* - John 5:45

In other words, Jesus is saying "You don't need me to condemn you. You already have one that condemns you. You put your trust in the law and that exposes it [condemnation] to you." Jesus is not a condemner. The sound of condemnation that you hear in your head can *never* be the Holy Spirit. His job is to glorify Jesus; not talk about sin. It is here where I believe that the church might have a backwards way of thinking as they inherently say "The Holy Spirit is convicting you of your sin." For that to be true, then the finished work of Christ on the cross had to have been in vain; null and void. Jesus was supposed to pay for all sins, what is the Holy Spirit doing pointing them out? The Spirit glorifies God, not sin. Any time that sin is spoken of, it gets way too much press in the life of a Christian. "So, why do I feel bad when I sin?" It's because you're better than that. You know better. The Spirit of God is reminding you of that truth- of your righteousness you have in Him as His child. You might be a child living like a hog, but thank God you're a child- His child. Get up, remind yourself of that and move on.

When you hear a message that cuts you down, fills you with shame, and puts condemnation between your ears, leave it. Get away from it. Flee. Still some might ask "Doesn't the Holy Spirit need to kick us around a little. Slap us on the wrist when we mess up?" No! Jesus got slapped by God so that we would never have to. He was chastised for our peace. My question to those is "Who do you think you are that you think your sin can surmount the grace and sacrifice of God?" He paid the price for you so that there is now no condemnation for those that are in Christ Jesus. If you *ever* hear a teaching that ministers condemnation, then it's not ministering about who you are. Paul says in Philippians 4:8:

*"Finally, brethren, whatever things are true, whatever things are noble, whatever things are just, whatever things are pure, whatever things are lovely, whatever things are of good report, if there is any virtue and if there is anything praiseworthy—meditate on these things."*

The moment that you said yes to Jesus is the moment all of your junk was pulled out of you by the death of Christ and the Holy Spirit took its place and set up residence in your chest; and it sits there ready to do all the work for you. His job is to tell you how lovely Jesus is and how much He loves you (*"and hope does not disappoint, because the love of God has been poured out within our hearts through the Holy Spirit who was given to us."*- Romans 5:5) and to tell you how righteous you are in Him no matter how unrighteous you may think you are by your actions.

The Spirit knows that the more you know you're righteous, the more righteousness comes out in your actions. This is a danger to the devil, because, if Christians knew how righteous they are by the finished work of Christ, then they would go into the world, not fearing the world at all. The fears of the world would diminish. Sin no longer is master over us. Death will lose its sting. In other words, we realize that the victory has already been won. The devil and his schemes are under our feet. We are more than conquerors through the finished work of Christ. The Holy Spirit witnesses for us, on our behalf, to God. What was He a witness to? He witnessed Christ on the cross, being broken, cursed, and chastised for your sins. God punished Jesus so He wouldn't have to punish you. Hebrews 10:15-17 says it beautifully what the Holy Spirit is a witness to and wants to remind you of every single day.

*"And the Holy Spirit also testifies to us; for after saying,*

*"THIS IS THE COVENANT THAT I WILL MAKE WITH THEM AFTER THOSE DAYS, SAYS THE LORD: I WILL PUT MY LAWS UPON THEIR HEART, AND ON THEIR MIND I WILL WRITE THEM,"*

*He then says,*

*"AND THEIR SINS AND THEIR LAWLESS DEEDS I WILL REMEMBER NO MORE."* **Hebrews 10:15-17**

In other words, every single day that you are a believer in Jesus, the Holy Spirit continually says "Hey kid, He remembers your sins no more. You're righteous and holy. He was beaten so that there would be no condemnation for you. You're loved so much - so, so much." That will glorify Jesus and the Spirit can start to go to work. If you don't understand that, and don't rest in the finished work of Christ, you don't have to get "re-dedicated" or "re-saved". I'm not even implying that you are lost. I'm saying that you have become ignorant to how righteous you are in the Lord.

The Holy Spirit convinces you of your righteousness. That's how He deals with you. Never will the Holy Spirit kick you around. He will only minister to you, what is true about you. He might say something like "You are the righteousness of God in Christ. You are a child of God. You are Christ in you, right now. You're holy, redeemed, delivered, forgiven." But, by the very grace of God with you, you will be empowered to fight. The fight to remember who you are in Him. The fight to constantly remember your position in Christ; a joint heir with Jesus. Concerning this, you won't have to be sin conscious - constantly having to work at sinning less and acting better. Being focused on Christ and who God's made you will inevitably enable you to refrain from sin and walk according to the Spirit in you as you rest in Him.

I'm not telling you to sit on your hands and do nothing as the Spirit of the living God is in you. I'm encouraging you to let the grace of God fight against sin, the principalities of darkness, and those spiritual forces that desire your demise. Paul says in Romans 5:20, *"where sin increased, grace abounded all the more"*. When you feel defeated, exhausted, fatigued and depressed by sin, realize at that moment, grace super abounds for you to accept and use against the evil one.

I understand, too that there has been some great debate over the 16th chapter of John concerning the conviction of the Holy Spirit. I grew up thinking that when I messed up and felt bad, then that was the Holy Spirit convicting me of my sins. As I began to understand who Jesus is, I began to find the incredible details of His character in the form of the Holy Spirit; and the conviction of my sins was absent in regards to the Holy Spirit's function in my life. The Spirit convicts the world of three things. Three different people are mentioned in the text below and I think it's extremely important to put this verse into context when reading. The Spirit convicts the sinners of their unbelief; saints of their righteousness; and Satan because he has already been judged.

*"And He, when He comes, will convict the world concerning sin and righteousness and judgment; concerning sin, because they do not believe in Me; and*

*concerning righteousness, because I go to the Father and you no longer see Me; and concerning judgment, because the ruler of this world has been judged.* - John 16:8-11

Notice when Jesus says that He (Holy Spirit) will come and convict the world of sin because "they" do not believe in me. I find it interesting how the term "they" is mentioned. It can only be referring to one set of people; unbelievers ("because they do not believe in Me"). Christ's sacrifice paid for everything except unbelief. Every behavioral sin that you have ever committed or will ever commit has been erased from your record for all time. The sacrifice of Jesus is sufficient and perfect. When dealing with sin, however, the Holy Spirit will convict unbelievers of their unbelief. Never can the Holy Spirit convict you of your sins as a believer after Christ has already paid for all of them for all time (Hebrews 10:17). In verse 10 of the above passage, it says:

*"and concerning righteousness, because I go to the*

*Father and you no longer see Me"* - John 16:10

The primary function of the Holy Spirit is to convict (or convince) believers of their righteousness ("because I go to the Father and you no longer see Me" –John 16:10). The Holy Spirit does not see sin, but purity and holiness. It is impossible for the Spirit of God in you, the hope of glory, to expose something that has already been taken care of by the blood, death, burial, and resurrection of Christ. May I present to you that the Spirit of God would be unholy and unrighteous if that were the case. God would result in being a liar and a fake if He were to say "Their sins and lawless deeds will I remember no more" and point out every wrongdoing that we have unfortunately done. The beauty of the Holy Spirit in us, as believers, is that not only are we forgiven for all time, but the Spirit testifies to us and convinces us of that every breath we take as new creations in Christ. I believe that perhaps the reason we need the Spirit to convince us of our righteousness is because we no longer see Jesus and it is easy for us, if it were left up to us, to remind ourselves of how righteous we are in Him. I know, for me personally, it is difficult and sometimes I fall victim to forgetting the truth about me and my identity in Christ. The Spirit, on the other hand will never let me forget that if He has anything to do with it.

*"and concerning judgment, because the ruler of this world has been judged."*- John 16:11

The last person that this passage addresses, is satan; the prince of the world (John 12:31). He has already been judged and will be thrust into the lake of fire for eternity. It is very bad news for the accuser of humanity. Not only do I not envy him, but I have overwhelming victory over him, through Him, who loved me and gave Himself up for me (Romans 8:37).

I find it interesting in the 8th chapter of the gospel of John, Jesus calls Himself the "Light of the world" immediately after He tells the woman caught in adultery "neither do I condemn you. Go and sin no more." I realize that John 8:11 ends one story and John 8:12 signifies a new one. However, I do think it's important to note that the Light of the world is not shining on condemnation, or shame, or punishment; rather it shines bright on no condemnation. This amazing gift of no condemnation came at a price though, and it challenges the mindset that perhaps most of us have grown up with. Jesus was beaten so that we would never be beaten. Christ was naked so we would always be clothed with His robe of righteousness. He was made poor so that we may be made rich. Curse fell upon Him so that we would be blessed. He was broken so that we would be healed and whole. Christ was forsaken so that we would never experience such distance from the Father. Christ paid for our sins so that we may be partakers of His righteousness. To think that He would do it all for us ragamuffins seems to be a ridiculous claim-unless of course it's true. Maybe Jesus is just that good. Maybe He really does love us that much. Maybe His love is so deep that it requires nothing in order to obtain it. Maybe He loves you so much that He decided to be made into the deepest darkest secrets that we each have, so that His light might shine righteousness through us. Ah, now that's some grace. That's a gift you don't deserve that you'll never have to pay for. Grab it, accept it, and hold onto it like the prized possession that you are, and that it is. It's yours for the taking.

Live free, Rest Easy,

Ben

# 9

# God Does Not Need Me

Dear Friend,

    I ventured to Indianapolis this weekend to hang out with my extended brothers and sisters in Christ. All I can say is that I'm so thankful for the One who saved me. He adopted me when I thought I was "un-adoptable". He accepted me when I couldn't even look at myself in the mirror. He forgave me even when I mocked Him and violated Him. He loved me when love was the furthest thing from my vocabulary. He healed me when I had wasted away my physical body. He decided to exchange my dead spirit with His alive, and powerful Spirit. He desires me, wants me, but He does not need me. Jesus wants me, He does not need me. Thinking on that brings tears to my eyes- He really does love me. When I learned that Jesus loves me with no strings attached; when I learned that Jesus doesn't need me, but so desperately wants me, it turned my heart into a puddle of putty (yes, I really said that). I feel His powerful spirit, coursing through my veins.

Much of these last months, I have been filled with nothing but shame, lies, and condemnation. Believing lies about who I am, I felt weak and my focus was not on Christ, but on other meaningless things. It was unhealthy and exhausting. I don't recommend it. Christ loves wooing us to Himself. In the midst of trouble, Christ is always there, even when you can't feel it. That does *not* change the fact that on my worst day, Christ is in me holding me, encouraging me, loving me, desiring me. That, is my Daddy. I was asked the question this weekend "What do you want to do more than anything else?" I gave the "Jesus" answer without even thinking. I said "I wanna tell people about Jesus". As I was driving to Indianapolis, I was praying and discovered that in fact all I wanna do is tell people about Jesus. I'm so proud to call Him mine. I'm so in love with Him. I'm crazy about Him. If everything else fails, I have Jesus.

As I sit here writing this note, I'm torn. I feel like Paul in Philippians 1:21-24, "For to me to live is Christ and to die is gain. But if I am to live on in the flesh, this will mean fruitful labor for me; and I do not know which to choose. But I am hard pressed from both directions, have the desire to depart and be with Christ, for that is much better; yet to remain on in the flesh is more necessary for your sake." I terribly desire to go the Father. I want to be there more than I want to be here. However, while this body is functioning properly, I can think of nothing else more productive than telling people about this Jesus, my Daddy. What an honor! It's not up to me for people to accept or not accept Him. What I can do, is tell people about this gift of abundant Life (John 10:10). I can tell people about this life changing grace. Grace is an undeserved, unmerited gift that you don't have to pay for. In terms of your salvation, the only requirement of grace is accepting it. It would make no sense if someone builds you your dream house with everything in it and simply tells you to move in. Then, you continue to try and pay for this free house. Jesus loves you so much that He created that dream house for you and wants you to move in, free of charge. Simply, move in and become the righteousness of God in Christ.

I know some will say that they have to get their act together before they can even begin to think about God. I was one of those people. I tried to work it out on my own so God would be pleased with me. I wanted to somehow show Him that I could kick the habit on my own. It never worked longer than a day or so. One day when I was laying in my loft, in a drunken stupor, that I realized I had nothing to offer God except my junk. I prayed that night for God to show Himself to me, to help me stop drinking, to heal me, to make Himself known. I was depressed, and messed up, but I experienced, firsthand, the grace of God. Though, it would be three years before I would connect the dots as to what really took place that night. He showed me that He didn't want me all fixed up. God wanted me just as I was. God wanted to heal my depression and broken heart. Can you believe it? Jesus wants you, even on your worst day! He loves you and desires you – He even likes you. Although it's tough at times to let go of life's issues, Jesus could not be happier when you do and place it in His hands.

Live Free, Rest Easy,

Ben

# 10

# Theology or Environment

Dear Friend,

In my opinion, some see grace as just a theological position. They talk religiously and hold their Bible under their arms and speak knowledge of grace without trusting it to govern their lives. There is one thing of which I am fairly certain. It is that if people realized they can live in grace, not just discuss a position on it, the church would have a different complexion. Unfortunately, some churches do not explain how to live in the freedom grace offers. They see grace as coupled with works or self effort. The new Covenant we have with Christ is brilliant and unconditional that it seems too good to be true. Because of human nature and performance-based society, we try to add to grace in an effort to understand it better.

But this "grace alone" seems to be a new concept. It certainly is not new. Perhaps we haven't rested in it, in order to experience it in our lives. There is a place where it is not necessary to rely on ourselves. The emphasis is not on our self efficacy. In this environment of grace we rely solely Him. The Holy Spirit is our counselor in us in times of need. In the authentic environment of grace, we can be naturally vulnerable. We need love, support, and affirmation and with Christ, we receive these things. Then we start to love authentically, without masks, in return. We get to live out of what is true about us - holy and righteous. Freedom finds its way into who we are. The theology of "I must do something to earn grace" or "I like grace, so what do I need to do to keep grace around" is ridiculous based on the way the Bible appropriates grace. Our finite minds may not understand that there is nothing we can do to earn grace and be loved more by God. There is nothing you can do to make God love you more or less; you did nothing to make Him love you in the first place.

Nonetheless, this does not mean that all we have to do is trust and love Him and kick our feet up and do nothing. However, look around at those truly basking in this environment of grace. People may not be perfect all the time in their behavior, but the Holy Spirit is at work in them; as a result the fruit of the Spirit is made manifest in them. As new creations in Christ, we share the grace that was so freely given to us.

Doesn't grace sound amazing? Aren't your ears tickling right now just at the thought of it? God doesn't hold any sin against us. You can begin to live as who God says you are, who we are in Him. However, when we inevitably make unhealthy decisions, the Holy Spirit in us tugs at our hearts and says "dear dear child, you're holy, righteous, justified, and sanctified. Don't forget that." There is no condemnation. There is repentance and confession that seems to flow naturally out of a new adopted child of God.

It is impossible to sin and not feel bummed out and broken. Those feelings aren't God's way of saying "straighten up". Rather, acts of disobedience contradict who we are in Him as His children. Sin is unnatural and foreign. It's almost as if we are walking around the deck of a proverbial pool. We are functioning just fine, breathing and enjoying some rays. Heck, we might even jump into the shallow end of the pool and splash around a bit. Perhaps we get some goggles and dive under water to see what it's like below the surface. We're going along just fine under water until 45 seconds lapse. Uh oh. All of a sudden, this neat view under water is now uncomfortable and our instinct is to gasp for air. When we swim to the surface, we experience what we were created to do; breathe. No one tells you that you need to breathe. Just like we don't have to think about breathing, a Christian doesn't have to think about walking in the Spirit; it's a natural occurrence. Life flows from God, fills the heart of a saint, enabling them to live out of their new nature. We can hold our breath (i.e. walking after flesh), but it's unnatural and won't last long. We will *always*, as saints, suck in the breath of Life. We don't naturally like sin when we get replaced with a new nature, a new identity. Our new nature changes who we are, Christ in us. This is how we can know we have been forgiven once for all.[1] A repentant heart is evidence.

Will you join me in this environment of grace? It will change your perspective on grace and bring freedom into your life. It's time to live under grace.

Live Free, Rest Easy,

Ben

# 11

# The Power of Authenticity

Dear Friend,

There was a time in my life, and sometimes even still, when I feel broken, torn down, ashamed, and regress to putting on a proverbial mask that says "I'm ok". I would put on the mask of "everything is fine" while possessing big smile, sad eyes, and no one wanted what I had. I soon realized that when I put on that mask, only my mask was getting loved. The deep desire for love in my soul got tossed in the back seat with all of the trash and unimportant things in life. I was aching for something true. I was scared of the potential responses I would get if I were to be known and revealed. Below is a letter of raw authenticity to the One, Jesus, who saved this life I tried to kill.

*Hey Jesus,*

*It's been a while since I've written You. What I'm about to write You, You already know, but here it goes. I need You. My behavior sucks right now and I detest it. I can't help but detest sin, especially when I choose to sin. I need help resting in You. I need help using the tools You have given me to fight the good fight. I want You to help me fight the good fight. I want You to help me focus on You more. I'm scared. I'm exhausted. I'm under attack. I'm tempted. Help me to realize everyday that You reside in me, and love me. I need Your help to prevent my old patterns from being a roadblock from You shining through me. Use me for Your glory. I know I'm not perfect in the flesh; but I know that You are and that You live in and through me. Help me realize this and take hold of this every day.*

*Lord, my focus is skewed more often than not. I am terribly sorry that I don't always live as the righteous and loved one You say I am. You tell me that I'm Yours: righteous and holy. When my behavior contradicts that, I feel like crap. It's that love that You love me with that makes me yearn for You. I know I have free will, and my free will chooses You, desires You, and wants to love You more than I did yesterday. I want to love You more than I am loving You right now. God, thank You for the cross. Thank You for forgiving me. Thank You for saving the life I was obliterating. Thank You for residing in me. Thank you for giving me You, at any time. You're all I need, all I want. Help me to understand the reality of having an extraordinary God in me. Your grace is sufficient; help me rely on it and use it to stand. I can't wait to be home soon. I want to see You. I want to feel Your arms around me. Thanks for Your love, mercy, and grace.*

*Your son,*

*Christ in Ben*

Grace- that sweet eloquent word we use that sounds like a soothing melody in our ears- is not just that we can be free of legalism, moralism, law, and ought. The greatest gift of grace is not that we can become new kind of legalist where we focus on who can dish out grace better than others or how much we can comprehend grace.

Maybe, just maybe, the greatest gift of grace, besides salvation, is authenticity. A friend of mine once confided in me by telling me that they didn't want to known. She told me, "I know who I am. I'm scared of getting found out. It scares me to risk being known. If people only knew the real me I would be ruined."

A performance-based realm is a cesspool for the Pharisee, who are known for their lack of authenticity and cleaning "the outside of the cup"[1] while the inside smells of death. In the American culture, the word "Pharisee" is well associated with words like "fake, religious bigot, resentful, angry, judgmental, hypocrite." Unfortunately, there are many who claim Jesus within the church walls and walk around as if they have spinach in their teeth and no one is saying anything. They are neither known, loved, nor are they liked by the non-religious.

I told my friend that eventually people would see the *real* them even if they were blinded to it. However, it was up to them to find a safe place of love and realness where protection and trust are available to be utilized whenever they desired. It's a healthy place where people will love you regardless of your junk. I chuckled and told my friend, "Look at me. I'm a goof. I'm weirdly unique and have messed up in the past, but I'm known. I'm revealed. I'm loved." It is becoming much clearer that when I resolve to be authentic, the more freedom I get to experience to be who I really am. Authenticity provides the avenue of boldness to the throne of grace in our times of need. The greatest place in the world to go in times of need is His throne of grace. It is here where we receive the vision and display of "where the worst of us can be known and find that we would be loved more, not less in the telling of it".[2]

In our desire to be in communion with God and be authentically true, we find rest and grace with Him. We are free to be open about our flaws with humans because even God Himself looks on them and says, "Yeah...so?" If He in His judgment seat has such a response, who are they to say otherwise? This is not to say that being authentic will never lead to us being judged by man- it absolutely will. But, His grace saves the day. We can rest because we know who we are, even when other people don't. Their opinions do not change our reality. Grace enables authenticity to infiltrate relationships and environments where we find ourselves at the end of the day liberated and encouraged that the worst of us is known and no one is leaving or loving us any less.

Love much, Rest easy,

Ben

# 12

# Who Are You?

Dear Friend,

Jesus said that He came that we may have life and have it abundantly. This verse seemed to resonate within my heart when I was in the great state of Alaska on a summer hike-a dream trip through the southern mountains. When I reached Byron Glacier, I thought to myself, "This is what it's all about. This is some serious abundance of everything good, pure, and holy." I had a massive blue glacier in front of me, mountains on either side, and a beautiful display of a glacier fed lake behind. For the first time in my life I was speechless. Tears were welled up in my eyes, and I felt like I was under an unstoppable force overwhelming me with goodness. As I sat on a rock and ate some trail mix, that one September night when I learned about grace replayed over and again in my head. Only this time it was a part that I had overlooked many times before.

His blood and forgiveness are sufficient, and you are now no longer under condemnation, but under favor, love, and grace. Though, there is much more than merely being forgiven from all your sins. If all that took place at the cross was just mere forgiveness, then I suppose that the naysayers that say "you can sin freely because God's forgiveness covers it all" would have a point. For example, if a prostitute is told that they are forgiven forever, would that make them stop prostituting themselves? Probably not. On the contrary, it might spur that lifestyle on if they knew they would never reap negative consequences of their choices. You see, in order for someone to change the way they live, there has to be an internal change. This is where the

Gospel goes to a whole new level. My friend, there was an incredible exchange that took place at the point of conversion (when you said "yes" to God). First, you have received Christ's righteousness and gave up your sin.[1] You receive a new eternal dwelling place in heaven rather than the torment in hell.[2] You are placed in peace with God and stand in His grace instead of standing condemned.[3] You are no longer dead inside, but have received a new Spirit.[4] The law that once held you in condemnation and shame has since been replaced with a new law leading you by grace.[5] He takes away weakness and gives His strength and power. [6] He discarded your impurities, and inserted His purity. [7] The redemption of God overwhelms and erases the hopelessness experienced when outside of Christ.[8] You now have peace, victory, joy, hope, fullness, goodness, love, kindness and forgiveness in the areas that were once plagued as tribulation, defeat, sorrow, despair, emptiness, evil, loneliness, and bitterness.[9] Perhaps the greatest changes come in the way of the releasing of the bogged down feelings of spiritual unrest, bondage, lies, insecurities, and the fear of judgment. And with that, the feeling of never being good enough or able to please Him enough.[10]

Liberated after accepting this truth, I was overjoyed with a strong desire to do a million jumping jacks just because I could. However, as I sat back and really examined what I had learned and accepted to be true, I asked myself the question, "Is knowing who you are enough? Is just the mere knowledge of my identity sufficient to live this abundant life?" There is distinct difference in knowing something and truly believing something. Knowing is based on logic, while belief is found in the depths of the heart. While an understanding of who you are in Christ supplies the tools needed to begin living abundantly, though "faith without works, is dead".[11] Basically, it profits you absolutely nothing to accept this truth then at the same time sit on your hands and tell no one about it. The natural response to this life changing, liberating truth is to bask in it, expose it to others, and share the message of Christ in you.

After all, if you're an apple seed and you get planted and your farmer waters you, takes care of you, and enables you to grow; you then mature into what is already true about you - an apple tree. Since you are alive, it is natural for you to produce fruit. You can't help but produce fruit. The farmer nurtured you, cared for you, and helped you grow along the way. You're a tree and that's your purpose, that's why you were planted, that's why you exist. Because you're a tree, you produce fruit. You are not fruit trying to prove to people that you are a tree.

I'm assuming you know that the farmer is Christ and He is the one that is making the plant grow. He is doing all the work. The waters of grace get poured out on you and you grow and mature and naturally produce fruit. It has nothing to do with anything you're doing. You get to rest in Him. I think a lot of people are out trying to collect apples in an attempt to show the world that they are a plant, instead of just existing and maturing into what is already true about them. Our faith in Christ naturally has works attached to it, because we are His children and workmanship created to do good works, why? Because we are *already* His. We cannot work our way into His adoption process. The works we do should never be an attempt to prove our faith, but rather they are open displays of what is true about us, since it could be argued that the human race has been tuned to performance-based behavior. I'm not saying that we are justifying ourselves before God through works, but helping those around us to understand who He is through our works.

I'd like to paint an appropriate picture of the details that take place at the point of a conversion. When converted, our old self, sin nature, Adamic nature, old man, dies and a new self, nature, desires, and repentant heart, resurrects. The Apostle Paul, author of the book of Galatians, states an important reminder regarding what happens at the point of a conversion. Paul says that "it is no longer I who live, but Christ lives in me" (Galatians 2:20). This is vital to remember as it speaks to your identity; who you are in Him.

The only person that has the power to resurrect is Christ. Our sins were crucified on the cross with Him. He became sin for us, died on the cross, and defeated death by raising from the dead so, as new creations, we no longer have our old dead self.[12] Consequently, everything comes from Him.

That day on the glacier in Alaska, when all of this played over in my head, tears of overwhelming joy streamed down my face. I realized that if I take things into my own hands, work on my junk, buck up, do better, or try to manage my sin, I am powerless and succeed in nothing other than changing behavior temporarily out of guilt or condemnation. This is contrary to what He desires for us. After all, in the gospel of John, Jesus said "I have come that they may have abundant life."[13] The abundant life rests in knowing who you are, and allowing the Spirit to shine through you.

How are we supposed to put this into action? In my previous mindset of working to please God, I would be ready to hear dutiful instructions the pastor had to give. I would do my best to get fired up and sold out as I would sit in the pew and search for new ways to make Him proud of me. Yet, knowing these truths about who He is, and about who I am in Christ I have to say: stop working to please God, and performing in order to have a closer relationship with Him - JUST STOP. PERIOD.

My encouragement to you, my friend, is to choose to rest completely in the sufficiency of Him. Working to do better, feeling a sense of guilt when you make inappropriate decisions-these are not from God. With the Holy Spirit, you have a Permanent Counselor constantly encouraging you and reminding you of your identity even after you have chosen and are confronted with sin.

As I wrote you before, the role of the Holy Spirit can never condemn you or convict you of your sins if in fact He resides in you. His role is to convince you that you are the beloved of Christ; to counsel you and be the mind of Christ in you, so that His hands and feet might not be ones of flesh but ones of the fullness of His power, so that His hands and feet might work and tread the entire earth. The role of the Holy Spirit is to glorify Jesus, not talk about sin. If that is the case, the Jesus' finished work is not a finished work. By "finished work" I'm talking about the sacrificial death that He incurred on our behalf. He was supposed to die for all the sins, so what is the Holy Spirit doing pointing them out? That is a backwards ideology in the modern church. When the Holy Spirit convicts you, it is not with any ounce of guilt or shame but with kindness; reminding you of who you are. So why do you feel bad when you sin? It's because you are better than that and the Holy Spirit in you is reminding you of that. You feel bad because you're an adopted child of the Living God acting like a slave. You don't have to be down and discouraged. If you mess up, get up and tell yourself that you're a child of God and move on. Let God begin to live through you, who Christ is in you, the hope of glory. Keep your eyes on Jesus and be sensitive to the Holy Spirit.

*"Jesus was made to be sin on our behalf so that we can become the righteousness of God in Christ"* (2 Corinthians. 5:21). This, my friend is something that we have got to constantly remember. We are not viewed in the eyes of God as being just positionally righteous.

For example, someone who receives an honorary doctorate degree simply means that they received the degree based on the invitation the school for them to come and receive it. Perhaps they have accomplished some great advances in the particular field the college specializes in or in life in general, etc. They can now call themselves a doctor. Most don't call themselves doctors however, because they didn't go through the process of paying their dues financially, writing and defending their thesis and dissertations and so on and so forth. Most churches today will view the members as being positionally righteous. Their mentality might sound something like "yes, you've been called righteous, but it's not actually real. God is somehow still very offended about our past mistakes. We're not really righteous, He just says we are."

If one is to believe this, then they have to change the complexion of the verse mentioned above to say that Jesus just carried our sins on His back when He was suffering on the cross. If Jesus' death was just positional, then those that believe in positional righteousness would have a point. But, the text doesn't say that. In fact the text (2 Corinthians 5:21) reads the *"He became sin"* so that *"we may be made"* righteous. I suppose one would have to ask themselves if they truly believe that Jesus was made to be sin at the cross;

and if the conclusion is a resounding "yes", then the back half of the verse is also ringing with truth.

You are wholly and wonderfully made; complete and righteous because Christ became the very essence of what God despises on your behalf. Paul, the author of the book of Corinthians explicitly states that Christ didn't die on the cross for His own sin, rather He had to be made sin itself so that we may be made the righteousness of God in Him. The crucifixion in the life of a believer is not a one way street that says "I've been crucified to sin, but sin has not been crucified to me and if I don't keep my faith strong enough, focused enough, or wise enough, then sin will come alive." In the book of Galatians, Paul says that, *"But may it never be that I would boast, except in the cross of our Lord Jesus Christ, through which the world has been crucified to me, and I to the world"* (Galatians 6:14). You are dead to it, and it is dead to you, so if you decide to go live in it; well that, my friend is just silliness.

However, there is a lot of preaching within the modern church that focuses on the old man to reform the old man. This is the main reason why Satan is doing his best to keep us focused on the old man. I have heard certain teachings that draws our attention the "old us" to improve our "old us". Perhaps this is why we are constantly getting told how to live. It's because most have difficulty believing that the old man is dead, gone, finished. They believe that the old man is not dead, only "covered". 2 Corinthians 5:14 says, "For Christ's love compels us, because we are convinced that ***one died for all***, and ***therefore all died***." [italics and bold mine for emphasis]. If Christ be dead, then we were all dead in Christ, which means that the old you is but now a distant memory. It's gone. In other words, the old you that existed before, died the moment you got saved.

Immediately wherever you were when you got saved, a brand new you began to exist. As soon as it did, the devil tried to get the new you to get rid of the old you. It doesn't make any sense does it? That he would try to get you to get rid of something that no longer exists? He does though. What he tried to do is get the church confused about being righteous by works to focus on the old you that is already dead, as if it weren't. The apostle Paul states that we should *"put off our former self"* (Colossians 3:9, Ephesians 4:22). What that is translated to is "STOP TALKING ABOUT HIM!" The more we start talking about him, the more he gets emphasized. The more he gets emphasized, the junk gets glory.

Unfortunately, some Christians in the church are looking forward to becoming a new creation. Paul said before in 2 Corinthians 5:14 we have something that constrains us, holds us together, compels us; the love of Christ in that when He died, so did we. You are now a new creation, my friend if you are a believer in Jesus Christ. The old you is dead, gone, finished. You are not being completed. You are complete. You are in the process, or being made complete. You are complete in Christ, you are a child of the living God.

People hear the words "complete forgiveness" and "no condemnation" and they instantly freak out. Some hear those words and think that everyone hearing those words will want to go out and sin. However, if we teach the complete message of once for all forgiveness with the truth that they have been divorced from the law and are now married to Christ through faith; no longer are you a servant but a child, there arises no reason to wallow in the former ways of life. Grace teachers seem to have gotten a bad name in some arenas. Perhaps it's because we got so amped up on telling people about His grace that we have ignorantly neglected to tell people about His exchange program. That is, that Christ is now your life and that He wants to live through you instead of you trying to do better things to make Him pleased with you. He wants to do the work so that you can rest.

This is victory. We can have this abundant life He freely gives to us right now. The emphasis on teaching legalism takes away from the simple act of following His lead, as He shows us the path of freedom. Allow Him to give us a piggy back ride through the issues that life sometimes brings. There will definitely be hard times where life gets messy, trying, downright depressing and overwhelming. Still, keep in mind that if your eyes are constantly on Him, things happen to flow in the right direction regardless of the particular season you find yourself in. Unresolved sin issues will start to fade.

My lunch came to a close with this contemplation as I gazed at Byron Glacier. To this day, it is my favorite spot in Alaska. I fondly remember that day as the one where Christ's love was made real to me- regardless of anything I did within myself or out of my ability and effort to be better. He loves us. Period.

Live Free, Rest Easy my friend,

Ben

# 13

# Freedom

Dear Friend,

I'm free. For a long time I sat and wondered what that meant. I'm free? Free from what? Free to do what? It sounds amazing, but, what does it mean for me? I heard the phrase "freedom in Christ" many time, but my understanding was that I was free to live by the law. No matter how hard I tried to get out, I was stuck. I wasn't free. I was a slave. As I write this, I can still remember crying because of the weight of all of it, keeping me from escaping the quicksand. I wanted to be released. I wanted to be *free*.

*"It is for freedom that Christ has set us free. Stand firm, then, and do not let yourselves be burdened again by a yoke of slavery."* - Galatians 5:1

We are called as believers to experience liberation and freedom. Correctly defining it has been a struggle for many within the confines of the church walls. When you say "yes" to Jesus being your Savior, you are free from ever having to try and perform your way out of hell and into heaven. As Jesus hung on the cross, He set us free from a multitude of things. He died to set us free from the penalty of sin-death. You are set free from condemnation. You are released from the law. You are set free from religion. You were once dead, but are now alive.

Perhaps one of the greatest things freedom brings is a new life. You have, living in you, the exact same Spirit that raised Jesus from the dead. Freedom simply says that you have something uniquely special about you that the world needs to know and you have the ability to expose it to them.

All too often, people bring back with their freedom,

the very thing they are free from - condemnation. No one should ever feel condemned or guilty for experiencing an abundant life in Christ, yet the evil one will make sure you feel ashamed of such a life. Unfortunately though, the devil works to get a Christian to experience guilt for such a life in an attempt to bring them back under law.

As believers, we get to share the incredible, life changing news to this generation that desires personal, authentic relationship. In Galatians 5:1, Paul says *"Stand firm, then, and do not let yourselves be burdened again by a yoke of slavery."* That yoke of slavery is the law - anything but the grace of the One who died a brutal death so you may live with Him forever. Paul desired the church at Galatia to stand firm in their freedom and never go back to the law in an attempt to justify themselves. Those who do such things have fallen from grace. If you try to justify yourself by your works, you will immediately go back under the curse that Christ died to take away from you - the curse of the law. The day you stop thinking about "doing" and focus on what He has done, the more freedom and liberty you get to walk in. The law exposed your sin but never gave you the answer to conquer it. Living free in Christ provides the guidance of the Spirit, and the power to walk in that freedom.

Adoption is very cool. It means that you were chosen for a new life and to be part of a family. I met my cat, Gracer, about a year ago. Two days before I was to take my annual trip to Alaska, a lady called me and asked me if I was interested in a cat. I have always been a strong advocate in the adoption of animals so I went to her house to see him. Adopted animals seem to have more of an appreciation than any I have been around. Gracer is a manx cat (he has no tail). He had been dropped off and had been outside for four months before we met. When inquiring about him, the lady said he was fixed and declawed. When thinking about a name that would best suit him, I went through an extensive search for names until the name Gracer stuck. Gracer needed relationship just like we all do. He needed love, just like us. My cat was in desperate need of a savior of sorts, of which we are in that same boat. As I was listening to music one night, Gracer decided to sit with me. He woke up and jumped off the top of the couch to where I was sitting. Without regard to my laptop being on my lap, he made his way to my lap forcing me to adjust what I was doing so he could lay on me. As I continued to focus on listening to music, talking to God and having communion with Him, I looked down at my cat. I'm not sure how long he was staring at me, but he was doing just that-looking me in the eye with a peaceful content look on his face. This made me smile. Soon, I began to see that Gracer is a great analogy for my relationship with God. It was two in the morning, a great time to worship I might add, when I began to understand this idea of adoption and new identity in Christ.

Gracer knows who he is. He understands his identity as a cat and he will boldly ask for food, water, love and anything else he might need. I can't help but think that this is just how we should approach our Daddy with everything we want and need. Hebrews 4:16 says that we can *"come boldly to the throne of grace, so that we may obtain mercy and find grace to help in time of need"*. I think so many times we see

God's personality as a law maker and neglect the fact that He is not just our Savior, but He in fact is our Daddy, Poppa, Father. The personal level of the relationship He desires for us all seems often too risky to trust and respond accordingly. Knowing the character of Jesus will enable that boldness to carry on and infiltrate our actions in regards to the relationship. As Gracer is able to come up to my lap any time he wants and just sit and stare contently into my eyes - it's a perfect display of the spiritual attitude with which we can approach our Daddy.

Another great thing God showed while worshipping that night had to do with rest. Gracer exhibits his rest (sleeps) more than he works. Yet, when Gracer is active, there's something within him that compels him to move, play, etc. I do not force him to play. I do not force him to do any labor. I do not make him act better or any of the like. Grace, as I sometimes call him, is motivated by something within him. God exposed to me the liberation that comes with resting. Of course being made up of body, soul, and spirit there are three types of rest that we can all experience. For our body, resting comes in the form of naps, relaxation of our bodies, or limited movement. Our soul takes up residence between our ears, in our brains. Since our soul is associated with our brain, personality, and feelings; learning about the One who died to save us, provides a liberating rest that would otherwise be absent. We can experience a high level of rest when we learn more about Him in our mind. And finally, spiritual rest. Resting spiritually is perhaps the most important type of rest that we can ever rely on. Spiritually, as believers, our rest has already been given to us through Him who loved us and died for us. In Matthew, Jesus said that whoever comes to Him, He would give them rest (Matthew 11:28-29). Our soul seems to wrestle with emotions. As our emotions have mountains and valleys, Jesus is constantly faithful even on our worst days when our behavior suggests that we are not; He is.

Gracer responds from what resides in him, his instincts that compel him to move. Christians have a new nature just like my cat has his own nature. It is my encouragement that you walk accordingly to what is true about you by being partakers of the divine nature that He has injected into you at the point of you saying "yes" to Him. I find it interesting that my tailless cat responds out of what resides in him yet sometimes I find myself doing the opposite.

*"So you should not be like cowering, fearful slaves. You should behave instead like God's very own children, adopted into his family—calling him "Father, dear Father." For his Holy Spirit speaks to us deep in our hearts and tells us that we are God's children. And since we are his children, we will share his treasures—for everything God gives to his Son, Christ, is ours, too. But if we are to share his glory, we must also share his suffering."* - Romans 8:15-17 New Living Translation (NLT).

This journey of freedom has been one that keeps bringing interesting revelations to me in weird, funky ways. Gracer can do anything he wants. I have never trained him except to use the litter box. I have never told him to "get down, stay off that, don't bite, etc", yet he refrains from all of it. Why? I think the reason is the same as like what Paul preached to us and to the churches of the New Testament. Paul in essence said to the Church, you have the Spirit of the living God in you and nothing you do; no behavior will make you any more or less righteous and holy. You are the righteousness of God in Christ. Christ lives in you. You are free to literally do anything you want and keep your holiness intact. But, I encourage you to remember who you are. You're a son of God. Sin does not master you. You're more than a conqueror. No, this is not some kind of passive aggressive way at behavior modification, but the way people respond to things is indicative most times of what they believe to be true about themselves. You're holy and have a new nature. Does my cat know he can do anything he wants? That nothing is binding him to rules and regulations? I'm not completely sure and refuse to go that deep into the mind of a feline. But, his responses and actions seem to be consistent with knowing me. I suppose yet another relation exists between Gracer and our freedom in Christ; knowing that we can do anything we want and still be righteous, yet we refrain from sin because we know who's we are (Gal. 4:5-6). I believe there is an incredible liberating Truth in the transformation that happens in the life of those that trust Him as their Savior. A friend of mine wrote "Knowing Christ empowers abundant life on earth, eternal life in heaven." Knowing Him really does change everything.

Rest Easy,

Ben

# 14

# The "Gamble"

Dear Friend,

I look at myself in the mirror sometimes and can't imagine anyone ever truly loving the person staring back at me. Jesus loves me, and He never loses the creativity in showing His love to me. Sometimes, He directs my focus to the cross. At other times, I'm in the middle of the mountains, canyons, or just driving down the road and His love is present. I can approach my heavenly Father with such boldness and confidence because He loves me - I'm His child (Galatians 4:6). Because He loves me, I can be real, authentic, and vulnerable and know He'll hold me in His arms every time. I think it's interesting how we define what things are because of their opposites. For example, we know what "up" is because we see "down". We know what "white" is because we see "black". We know what "North" is because we have "South". However, we don't know what "love" is because of "hate". No, perhaps the only time that we don't define what something is because of it's opposite is when it comes to love.

*"In this is love, not that we loved God, but that He loved us and sent His Son to be the propitiation for our sins...We love, because He first loved us." – 1 John 4:10,19*

It is difficult to fathom that He would desire to have a personal relationship with each of us. Seven billion people in this world and He wants intimate relationship with each individual? This is where Jesus gets good; buckle your seatbelt. Jesus has been persistent in wooing us back to Him even when we neglect Him. He loves us anyway. He *loves* me - Ben Ellard. The guy that has tattoos, loves rock music, recovered from an alcohol addiction, and is living in a remote town in the middle of Kentucky is loved by God. Not only does He love me, but He loves me in every way that He loves His Son (John 15:9, 17:23). The same can be said of you, my dear friend. I don't care about your sins, behaviors, or insecurities. His love trumps all of it.

God loves you, desires you, wants you, and is passionately crazy about you. He is fiercely, determined, and persistently wooing you to Him. It simply takes a "yes" from your heart to become this amazing new creature with His nature, power, and love in you, forever. It takes a humble "yes" from your heart to be sealed and justified for all time. It only takes a sincere "yes" for you to be forgiven forever, found not guilty, blameless, and beyond reproach. By saying "yes" to Him, then you can honestly be clean, pure, holy, alive, forgiven, new, beautiful, acceptable, complete, adored, chosen, adopted, able, intimately loved, desired, wanted, protected, enjoyed, secured, sealed, delivered, comforted, understood, known, righteous, redeemed, blameless, defended, valued, held, listened to, honored, lacking nothing, praised, appreciated, given sufficient grace, you are precious, never condemned, shamed, or punished. You are more than a conqueror. All of this because of God's love and grace.

Many churches give laundry lists of things you should and shouldn't do now if you are a Christian. I resolve this to do the opposite. I'm not going to give you a laundry list of things you should do. On the contrary, I'm going to give you a list of things you do not have to do in order to receive this precious Life and eternal salvation.

*"You don't have to fix yourself, clean yourself up, start going to church, talk religiously, change your friends, and stop swearing. You don't have to stop dancing. You don't have to tell all your secrets in a small group. You don't have to attend a small group. You don't have to become a right winged conservative. You don't have to be better, you don't have to promise*

*anything, you don't have to change squat! Because what God wants to change, He will change in you."*[1]

You will receive a new nature as mentioned before. You will receive a new desire to love Him, not an obligation to a God that will condemn you to hell if you don't do what He wants you to do every second of every day of your life. He will go to work on your heart, and in turn, you will be stripped down, raw, bare, and willing to put your life on the line because of the trust you have in Him. I've been ridiculed for this message because to some it seems like I'm light on sin; that you can go out and live engulfed in sin and be happy to know your sins are forgiven.

I need to make something abundantly clear. Grace is only accepted by faith. You have the capacity to say 'no' to Jesus and you will go to hell, but it won't be because of your cheating, lying, infidelity, cursing, addiction or destructive behavior. It will be because you said "no" to Jesus. Jesus explicitly says that there's one way home and that is "yes" to Jesus. And it's so easy, and beautiful. He even lets us know that if this is what we are committing ourselves to Him that His yoke is easy, and His burden is light.

Clarence Jordan, the author of the Cotton Patch Version of the Bible, perhaps said it best when he paraphrased Romans 6:1-2 when he writes *"So what are we advocating? Let's wallow in sin, so more grace may pour forth? Hell, no! How can we who died in sin still live in it?"* (Romans 6:1-2, Cotton Patch Version). In the book, "Bo's Café" my friend John writes,

*"Grace is a gift only the non religious can accept. They're the only ones who can use it. Religious folk see grace as soft so they try to manage their junk with their own will power and tenacity. Nothing defines religion quite as well as a bunch of people trying to do impossible tasks with limited power while bluffing to themselves that it's working."*[2]

Some may see grace as soft, and like a doormat you wipe your feet on before you enter the door. However, we're new creations and we don't want to take advantage. We have a new nature that falls in line with what God has desired for us all along. Grace in essence is the ability of God in you to do His will on a daily basis. It's core is strength, love, power, forgiveness and freedom.

Grace is mentioned over 100 times in the New Testament for a reason. This powerful word, *grace*, it's what Paul uses to *stand* in Romans 5:1-2. Even so, it is what Paul tells Timothy to be *strong* in in 2 Timothy 2:1. More so, grace is what God Himself says to Paul is *sufficient*, and will be perfected in times of weakness in 2 Corinthians 12:9.

I love this piece also written by my friend, John Lynch, called the "New Testament Gamble". John calls it the New Testament Gamble because in order to trust the words to be true, it could feel like a gamble to us. In this passage, it is as if God reveals everything, shows His cards, and provides you with His insight to what is really going on.

### *The New Testament "Gamble"*

*What if I tell them who they are? What if I take away*

*any element of fear in condemnation, judgment or rejection? What if I tell them I love them, will always love them? That I love them right now, no matter what they've done, as much as I love my only Son? That there's nothing they can do to make my love go away?*

*What if I tell them there are no lists? What if I tell them I do not keep a log of past offenses, of how little they pray, how often they've let me down, made promises that they don't keep? What if I tell them they are righteous, with my righteousness, right now? What if I tell them they can stop beating themselves up? That they can stop being so formal, stiff and jumpy around me?*

*What if I tell them I'm crazy about them? What if I tell them, even if they run to the ends of the earth and do the most horrible, unthinkable things, that when they come back, I'd receive them with tears and a party? What if I tell them that if I am their Savior, they're going to heaven no matter what—it's a done deal?*

*What if I tell them they have a new nature—saints, not saved sinners who should now 'buck up and be better if they were any kind of Christians, after all He's done for you! What if I tell them that I actually live in them now? That I've put My love, power, and nature inside of them, at their disposal?*

*What if I tell them that they don't have to put on a mask? That it is absolutely OK to be who they are at this moment, with all their junk. That they don't need to pretend about how close we are, how much they pray or don't, how much Bible they read or don't?*

*What if they knew they don't have to look over their shoulder for fear if things get too good, the other shoe's gonna drop? What if they knew I will never, ever use the word "punish" in relation to them? What if they knew that when they mess up, I will never "get back at them?"*

*What if they were convinced that bad circumstances*

*aren't my way of evening the score for taking advantage of me?*

*What if they knew the basis of our friendship isn't how little they sin, but how much they let me love them? What if I tell them they can hurt my heart, but that I never hurt theirs? What if I tell them I kind of like Eric Clapton's music too? What if I tell them I never really liked the Christmas hand bell deal with the white gloves? That the "thee's and thou's" have always bugged me? What if I tell them they can open their eyes when they pray and still go to heaven? What if I tell them there is no secret agenda, no trapdoor? What if I tell them it isn't about their self-effort, but about allowing me to live my life through them?[3]*

Is Jesus worth your trust? If you wish to ask Him into your heart, there is no "right way" to call out to Him. However, you may read the prayer below as a guide:

*"God, I receive your forgiveness in my life. I thank*

*You for adopting me and making me Yours. I trust you now as my Savior." – Amen*

A man of God by the name of Bob Warren said this, and it is my encouragement to you as well; "spend time enough, letting Him teach you enough, that you may know Him enough, to trust Him enough, to let Him live His life through you." I thank God for you, my dear friend.

Live Free, Rest Easy,

Ben

# Index

**The Cross**
1. Matthew 6:12; Luke 11:4

**The Beauty of Covenant**
1. Smith, M. (2006). *The power of the blood covenant: uncover the secret strength in god's eternal oath.* Harrison House.
2. Hebrews 10:12
3. Matthew 27:46; Mark 15:34
4. Ephesians 2:11-19

**Loving to Death**
1. Matthew 22:36
2. 1 Corinthians 2:2

**Sufficient Forgiveness**
1. Romans 5:6, 5:8, 5:10
2. Hebrews 10:17
3. Psalm 103:12, Isaiah 38:17, Isaiah 44:22, Jeremiah 31:34, Micah 7:19, Ephesians 4:32, Colossians 1:14,22, Colossians 2:13-14, I John 2:12

4. Ezekiel 36:26, Romans 5:19, 1 Corinthians 6:11, 2 Corinthians 5:17, Colossians 1:22, Galatians 2:20, Galatians 3:22, Galatians 3:27, 2 Timothy 2:21
5. John 3:16, Romans 6:11, Romans 6:23, 1 Corinthians 15:22, Ephesians 2:5, Colossians 2:13
6. Romans 10:17
7. Hebrews 10:17

**Gift of no Condemnation**
1. Colossians 3:3-4, Galatians 2:20, 2 Corinthians 5:17, Romans 6:6, Ephesians 2:6-10
2. Romans 8:1
3. 2 Corinthians 5:21
4. Hebrews 10:1-18

**Theology or Environment?**
1. Hebrews 10:12

**The Power of Authenticity**
1. Matthew 23:26-28
2. Quote by John Lynch

**Who Are You?**
1. 2 Corinthians 5:21
2. Ephesians 2:6,19
3. Romans 5:1

4. Galatians 2:20, Ezekiel 36:26
5. Romans 7:4-6
6. 2 Corinthians 12:9-10
7. Hebrews 10:21-22
8. 1 Corinthians 1:30
9. Ephesians 2:14, 1 Corinthians 15:57, John 15:11, Colossians 1:27, Colossians 2:9-10, Galatians 5:22, 1 John 4:16, Colossians 2:13, Galatians 5:22
10. Hebrews 4:10, John 8:36, John 8:32, Ephesians 1:6, 1 John 4:17, Galatians 5:24, Romans 8:1
11. James 2:26
12. Romans 6:6
13. John 10:10

**The Gamble**
1. Spoken from a sermon by John Lynch on February 22, 2009
2. Lynch, J, Thrall, B, & McNicol, B. (2009). *Bo's café*. Hodder & Stoughton.
3. Thrall, B, McNicol, B, & Lynch, J. (2004). *Truefaced: trust God and others with who you really are*. Navpress Pub. Group.

Made in the USA
Lexington, KY
14 December 2011